# One More Time

# One More Time

*Harlem Renaissance History
and Historicism*

**Richard A. Long**

*For Luther and Callie
Peace
and pleasant voyages

Richard*

The FIRE!! Press
Elizabeth, New Jersey
2006

*The FIRE!! Press*
*241 Hillside Road*
*Elizabeth, New Jersey 07208*
*fire.press@verizon.net*
*http://firepress.com*

*For Eleanor Traylor*

# Contents

# Foreword

The continued and growing fascination of the Harlem Renaissance for a wide public is not without hazard for serious students. Inevitably the emergence of elaboration and distortion make a call for sobriety and correction necessary. The three essays offered here grow out of an impulse to keep the history—and hence the historiography—of the Harlem Renaissance in focus.

The first essay was written for a proposed collection which failed to materialize as a publication. In this essay I felt the need to assert the organic position of the Harlem Renaissance in African American culture, in opposition to implications of its eccentricity, and to illustrate the assertion with references to the complex career of James Weldon Johnson, an icon of African American culture and a mentor of the Harlem Renaissance.

The second essay which muses upon historiography was delivered as the forty-eighth Charles Eaton Burch Memorial Lecture at Howard University on April 8, 1999. Initiated in 1949, the Burch Lecture was established by the English Department to commemorate Professor Burch, a Defoe scholar, who exemplified the highest ideals of humanism and collegiality. Howard's English Department has a noble legacy which includes such predecessors of Professor Burch as Benjamin Brawley; such contemporaries as Sterling Brown and

Arthur P. Davis; and such successors as Charlotte Crawford Watkins and Eleanor Traylor.

The third essay was presented at Emory University during the year preceding my retirement. It was conceived as a further reflection on the terrain explored in the Burch lecture.

RAL

# I

# Roots of the Harlem Renaissance: The Example of James Weldon Johnson

The Harlem Renaissance, unlike Athena, did not spring from the cranium of an unsuspecting deity; rather it is rooted firmly in and was a response to the history and existence of African Americans. Two recent trends in scholarship, both meritorious, need guidance and correction from a probing of the African American roots of the Harlem Renaissance. One such trend, the project of relating the Harlem Renaissance, its personalities and thematics to the larger expanse of contemporary American culture, is exemplified in the work of Ann Douglas and George Hutchinson.[1] The other noteworthy trend is the exploration of international connections and resonances of the Harlem Renaissance explored in the exhibition and catalogue *Rhapsodies in Black*.[2]

Both trends take some account of motifs which figure prominently in the Harlem Renaissance; they require a realization that the motifs emerge from the fabric of the

---

1 Douglas, Ann. *Terrible Honesty: Mongrel Manhattan in the 1920's* (New York: 1995); George Hutchinson, *The Harlem Renaissance in Black and White* (Cambridge, Massachusetts, 1995).

2 *Rhapsodies in Black: Art of the Harlem Renaissance (Berkeley, California: 1997).*

pre-Harlem Renaissance African American experience. The most persistent motif is that of the quickening effect of cityward migration which resulted in the rapid development of urban Black communities, particularly Harlem, following World War I, and the resulting cultural innovations. A second motif is the presence of race consciousness, seen by some as verging on nationalism, by others merely as an assertion of an essential identity. This motif is explored exhaustively (perhaps with contradictions) in Alain Locke's contributions to *The New Negro*.[3] Closely related to this motif is the conundrum of representation. When does humor become caricature? When is realism calumny? A third motif also explored if not fetichised in Locke is the significance of folk tradition in artistic creation. Finally there is the motif of ancestral Africa which reverberates as melancholy in Countee Cullen's poem "Heritage," [4] and with triumphalism in the oratory of Marcus Garvey.[5]

These four motifs, migration, race consciousness, the folk tradition, and Africa, can be perceived as continua, reflections and distillations of the panorama of African American history, resonating with familiarity. This panorama is best displayed in terms of cultural epochs rather than in strict chronological terms. I designate these epochs as follows: the folk-rural, the folk-urban, and the trans-urban.[6] The folk-rural rises in the plantation setting

---

3   "The New Negro," et passim in *The New Negro*, ed. Alain Locke (New York, 1925; repr. 1992).

4   Published in *The New Negro* (pp. 250-53) not with other poems, but under the rubric "The Negro Digs Up His Past."

5   *The Philosophy and Opinions of Marcus Garvey*, ed. Amy Jacques Garvey (New York, 1923, 1925; repr. 1969).

6   A fuller presentation of cultural epochs than the one which follows may be found in Richard A. Long, *African Americans: A*

of the early eighteenth century in the upper South and persists in some form until the Great Depression of the thirties; the folk-urban is the creation of the ongoing migration of Blacks to cities beginning with that of freedmen and freedwomen following emancipation, and is superseded by the trans-urban epoch triggered by the Great Migration associated with the First World War. Within this paradigm the Harlem Renaissance may be viewed as an expression of the trans-urban epoch. Parallel to the folk-rural and the folk-urban epochs, and merging with the trans-urban, is the citadin culture characteristic of the old urban African American populace of the cities, a group which sought to conform to the norms of the city life surrounding them.

More particularly, the folk-rural culture, arising in the world of the plantation, saw the formation of most of the characteristic expressive forms associated with African American tradition. Religion emerged both as solace and a vehicle of hope for a better day. Within the arc of religion, superimposed Christian hymnody was complemented by the highly original Negro spiritual; the homily was transformed into the performative folk sermon. Song accompanied work and play. Verbal art in the form of proverb and the tale lent savor to daily life. The ending of slavery did little to modify this rural culture, which persisted to the decline of rural life in the United States in the period preceding World War II.

The folk-urban is the transmutation of this rural culture into the cities of the North and the South and is initiated by Black migration into the cities at the end of the Civil War, a movement away from the rural world which

*Portrait (New York, 1993), passim.*

was ongoing, but which was conditioned by continuing contact between city and country based on familial and other ties. The folk-urban sees a surge in popular congregational religious expression whose enthusiasm contrasts with that of the more sober church-going of the citadin population. It sees the development of new secular musical forms, culminating in early jazz and the blues, forms not welcomed by the citadin or older inhabitants. The conflict between the countrified folk-urbanities and their citadin compeers is one of the elements revealed in W. E. B. Du Bois's pioneering and classic sociological study of the 1890's, *The Philadelphia Negro*.[7]

It was the First World War which unleashed the Great Migration, the subject of considerable literature and folklore. The ending of immigration from Europe and the resulting labor shortage in an expanding economy was an open, if reluctant, invitation to African Americans to leave the South in great numbers for the cities of the North and the Midwest, increasing exponentially the Black populations of those cities and creating the trans-urban.

> Trans-Urban Culture is the result of the linking up of the new urban concentration of blacks across the country, South and North, East and West. The linkages were due largely to the ease of travel from city to city by rail, and in part to the developing technologies that were transforming the whole United States: the phono-

---

7  Du Bois, *The Philadelphia Negro* (Philadelphia, 1899; repr., New York, 1967).  Du Bois's study, while confined to Philadelphia, can be used as a template for understanding contemporary conditions in other cities such as New York/Brooklyn, Washington, D.C. and Chicago.

graph, motion pictures, and radio. For example, records brought Bessie Smith and other black entertainers into the homes of countless blacks throughout America's cities. It is interesting to notice, too, how many blues songs allude to train travel, and how much jazz sonorities and rhythms reflect the sound of the steam locomotive.[8]

Seen from the perspective of the cultural epochs that have been delineated, the Harlem community may be perceived as one of the new enclaves of the trans-urban epoch. In contrast with the cities of the Midwest and the South, however, but in common with other Eastern cities such as Philadelphia and Boston, the Black population of New York included immigrants from the Caribbean, particularly from the British West Indies. Significantly, by the mid-twenties, there were also Africa-born inhabitants in Harlem.

Alain Locke celebrates this new Harlem in his title essay "The New Negro."

> Here in Manhattan is not merely the largest Negro community in the world, but the first concentration in history of so many diverse elements of Negro life. It has attracted the African, the West Indian, the Negro American; has brought together the Negro of the North and the Negro of the South; the man from the city and the man from town and village . . . . Within this area, race sympathy and unity have determined a further fusing of sentiment and experience. So what began in terms of segregation becomes

---

8  Long, p. 67.

more and more, as its elements mix and react, the laboratory of a great race-welding.[9]

In *The New Negro*, W. A. Domingo examines the presence of people of Caribbean origin in post-World War I Harlem under the approving title, "Gift of the Black Tropics." Discussing the then often-discussed ill-feeling between those from the Caribbean and the natives, he presciently notes:

> It is to be expected that the feeling will always be more or less present between the immigrant and the native born. However, it does not extend to the children of the two groups, as they are subject to the same environment and develop identity of speech and psychology.[10]

The best overview of Harlem during the Renaissance and of the African American presence in New York from the beginnings of the city as New Amsterdam in the seventeenth century was and is a lively and genial book by James Weldon Johnson entitled *Black Manhattan*, published in 1930. Neither the texts nor the life of Johnson can be considered victims of neglect in Harlem Renaissance studies; however, they deserve to be more centered, for Johnson was not only one of the "elders" of the Renaissance, but also he is indispensable for an understanding both of the roots and the unfolding of the Harlem Renaissance. For the roots of the Harlem Renaissance one can profitably turn to two of his books, the novel *The Autobiography of An Ex-Colored Man* published in 1912 and the anthology *The Book of American Negro Poetry* published in 1922. In the unfolding of the

9  *The New Negro*, pp. 6-7.
10  Ibid., pp. 348-49.

Harlem Renaissance, we must note his books, *American Negro Spirituals* (1925, 1926), done in collaboration with his brother, J. Rosamund Johnson, and the collection of poems, *God's Trombones: Seven Negro Sermons in Verse (1927)*.

Prior to the publication of his novel, Johnson had already been an educator, a lawyer, a successful collaborator as lyricist in musical theater, as well as a member of the United States consular service in Latin America. In the novel, drawing upon his own experiences, he depicts the musical life of folk-rural culture, as well as the early New York jazz scene, as it developed in the precincts of the Hotel Marshall on West 53rd Street at the dawn of the century. The novel explores the question of the transformation of this musical material into the music of the concert hall, an obsession of Alain Locke and others during the Harlem Renaissance. Later in the decade, Johnson's sermon poem "The Creation" that appropriated folk verbal art showed the same concern for the black community already manifested in Du Bois's *The Souls of Black Folk* (1903). In the 1922 anthology, *The Book of American Negro Poetry*, Johnson provided by means of his introduction and selections the platform upon which the poetic enterprise of the Harlem Renaissance was constructed.

The dominant figure in African American poetry up until 1922 was Paul Laurence Dunbar, whom the young Johnson had met in 1893 at the beginning of Dunbar's career. In the late nineties Dunbar had blazed like a meteor in the bleak landscape of American poetry. By 1922, however, his achievement had dimmed in the light of the "new poetry" which began to be published around 1910, and which was produced by Robert Frost, Edward Arlington Robinson, Ezra Pound and the Imagists. John-

son held out the expectation that African American art-
istry would flourish in due time. His re-edition of his
anthology in 1931, following the Harlem Renaissance,
provided the confirmation of his prognosis.
Reverberating through Johnson's life and work prior
to the Harlem Renaissance we can distinguish all of the
motifs we have identified as characteristic of the Renaissance and thus see that these motifs are indeed develop-
ments of a rooted consciousness.

Johnson was born in 1871 in Jacksonville, a city in
Florida similar in history and social structure to the cities
of the deep South rather than to the younger semi-tropical
Miami. His parents had followed a migration path from
New York to the Bahamas to Florida, thus contributing to
his sense of migration as a phenomenon of African
American life. In his youth he was sent to study at the
preparatory school of Atlanta University in an emerging
metropolis of the deep South; he remained there for his
university studies. He returned to Jacksonville for several
years of professional employment as an educator and a
lawyer, migrating afterward in 1902 to New York City to
collaborate with his brother on songs for the musical
stage.

Johnson's race-consciousness, and indeed that of
many articulate African Americans of his generation,
was expressed while he was still an undergraduate at At-
lanta University in an 1892 prize oration, "The Best
Methods of Removing the Disabilities of Caste from the
Negro." [11] However, it is Johnson's text for the anthem
"Life Every Voice and Sing," written to be presented at a
Lincoln's Birthday celebration in 1900 and sung to the

---

11 Repr. in *The Selected Writings of James Weldon Johnson,* ed.,
Sondra Kathryn Wilson (New York, 1995), II, pp. 423-26.

music of brother J. Rosamond Johnson, which has become the most recurrent community expression of racial
pride and solidarity for African Americans: "Let us
march on till victory is won." [12]

Among Johnson's early poetry there are several poems in the mode of Dunbar which one might denominate
a conventionalized folk voice. Most notable among these
is "Sence You Went Away," published in 1900 in *The
Century Magazine* and subsequently taken to be an actual
folk piece by the unwary.[13]

Johnson had tapped the authentic folk voice by 1918
when he wrote the first draft of "The Creation," then entitled "Sermon on the Creation." It was published in 1920
and may be seen as a herald of the folk consciousness of
the Harlem Renaissance.[14]

Having made a brief case for looking at James Weldon
Johnson's life and work for more insight into the roots of
the Harlem Renaissance, it is important to assert that he is
also representative of a significant cohort of African
American intellectuals active in the early twentieth century. Among these were Du Bois; Carter G. Woodson,
historian and founder of the Association for the Study of
Negro Life and History; Jessie Fauset, teacher, poet and
scholar, later editor and novelist; Charles W. Chestnutt,
novelist and lawyer. All of these endured to make direct
contributions, as Johnson did, to the Harlem Renaissance.

---

12  Repr. in Eugene Levy, *James Weldon Johnson* (Chicago, 1973),
    pp. 71-72.
13  Repr. in *The Negro Caravan*, ed. Sterling Brown, et al. (New
    York, 1941, repr. 1970), p. 328.
14  Levy, p. 299ff.

# II

# Toward the Historiography of the Harlem Renaissance

The phrase *Harlem Renaissance* has superseded earlier terms, such as *New Negro Movement* and *Negro Renaissance*, as the designator of choice to characterize the artistic ferment among African Americans which became fully manifest in the mid-1920's. *Harlem Renaissance*, however, was not commonly used until the 1950's, propelled probably by its use in John Hope Franklin's *From Slavery to Freedom*. The term *Negro Renaissance* had been popularized by Alain Locke, who based it on the analogy of the term *Irish Renaissance* (also *Celtic Renaissance*) current as a descriptor for the Dublin-based Irish cultural movement centered around William Butler Yeats. Locke clearly perceived his "renaissance" as a nationwide phenomenon of which New York/Harlem was the capital. In broader terms this "renaissance" must be viewed as an aspect of the life of the early trans-urban era of African American culture. (Long, *Grown Deep*, p. vii)

The Harlem Renaissance has been primarily treated by literary historians and critics and therefore shows up on our screens most often as a literary movement, but there is an extensive panorama of Renaissance activity and thought which has over time evoked the attention of historians of society, art, music and other cultural phenomena.

Indeed it is the writings of several scholars from outside the domain of literary history which have marked most decisively the development of Harlem Renaissance studies. I refer specifically to John Hope Franklin, Nathan Huggins and David Levering Lewis.

Alain Locke had joyfully trumpeted to the world in 1925:

> The Younger Generation comes, bringing its gifts. They are the first fruits of the Negro Renaissance. Youth speaks, and the voice of the Negro is heard. (*The New Negro*, p. 97)

However, only five years later, he wrote:

> The much exploited Negro Renaissance was after all a product of the expansive period we are now willing to call the period of inflation and over production. . . . The second and truly sound phase of the cultural development of the Negro in American literature and art cannot begin without a collapse of the boom. . . . ("This Year of Grace," *Opportunity* 9 (February 1931): 48)

Thus we see it may have been Alain Locke who killed the Renaissance in 1930, and not the Depression. But we must note that in 1930 James Weldon Johnson published *Black Manhattan* and in his pages there is no such note of reserve, and in the next year Johnson issued the second edition of *The Book of American Negro Poetry* in which at least that aspect of Renaissance activity was perceived to be in good health. In 1937 two literary scholars, an older and a younger one, of different temperaments, looked back on the 1920's in literature and both were relatively reserved in their judgments of its glories. The older man was Benjamin Brawley, who published *The Negro Genius* in that year; the younger was Sterling Brown, who published two companion volumes, *The Negro in American Fiction* and *Negro Poetry and Drama*, in the Bronze Booklet series edited by Alain Locke. In 1939 the Harlem Renaissance writers were subjected to kinder scrutiny in a literary study by Saunders Redding, *To Make A Poet Black*; the title comes from a Countee Cullen sonnet.

In 1940, Langston Hughes published an autobiography, *The Big Sea,* tracing his life up to the early thirties. It is episodic in organization, and the last third of the volume carries the heading "Black Renaissance," the first section of which is entitled "When the Negro Was in Vogue." The opening paragraph is all Langston Hughes:

> The 1920's were the years of Manhattan's black Renaissance.  It began with "Shuffle Along," "Running Wild," and the Charleston.  Perhaps some people would say even with "The Emperor Jones," Charles Gilpin, and the tom-toms at the Provincetown.  But certainly it was the musical revue, "Shuffle Along," that gave a scintillating send-off to that Negro vogue in Manhattan, which reached its peak just before the crash of 1929, the crash that sent Negroes, white folks, and all rolling down the hill toward the Works Progress Administration. (*The Big Sea*, p. 223)

Hughes mentions in rapid order Roland Hayes, Paul Robeson, Florence Mills, Bessie Smith and Clara Smith (there was also Trixie Smith; Paul Oliver has said that anybody named Smith could find somebody to let them sing the blues). Hughes also talks about the Cotton Club and the Savoy. He then goes on to drop in the same sentence the names of Countee Cullen, Ethel Waters, Claude McKay, Duke Ellington, Bojangles and Alain Locke. It is safe to say that Hughes's lively depiction is a stellar moment in the myth of the Harlem Renaissance and in its historiography.

The killjoy Alain Locke, from his critical perch in *Opportunity*, noted that Hughes's experiences "are not plumbed to any depth of analysis or understanding, with the possible exception of Washington society." He goes on to say,

> If, as in this case, righteous anger is the mainspring of an interest in social analysis with Langston Hughes, one wishes that more of life had irked him. ("Of Native Sons: Real and Otherwise," *Opportunity* 19 [January/February 1941] repr. Locke, *Critical Temper*, pp. 301-02)

Locke pointedly does not comment on the depiction of the "Black Renaissance," by Hughes, a depiction which was to entrance a generation of younger readers and writers. One may suspect that this depiction was not without an impact on the sober account given in John Hope Franklin's *From Slavery to Freedom*, which appeared in 1947 and which has a section entitled "A Harlem Renaissance." At any rate, this is a significant moment in historiography, for the term *Harlem Renaissance* is here dispatched on its merry and conquering way.

Alain Locke died in 1954. The next year the Sixteenth Annual Spring Conference of the Division of the Social Sciences at Howard University was devoted to his memory under the theme title, *The New Negro Thirty Years Afterward*. The conference thus also marked the thirtieth anniversary of the publication of *The New Negro*. The contributors included Arthur Huff Fauset, Charles S. Johnson and Horace Kallen; and from the Howard faculty, Sterling Brown, Emmet Dorsey, John Hope Franklin, E. Franklin Frazier, Eugene C. Holmes, Rayford W. Logan, Robert E. Martin and James A. Porter. The contributions which are of greatest interest to our historiography are those of Johnson, Brown and Porter.

Johnson, who as editor of *Opportunity* had really engineered Alain Locke into his role as mentor of the Renaissance, entitled his piece, "The Negro Renaissance and Its Significance." Looking at the Renaissance, after paying respect to the presence of Du Bois and James Weldon Johnson, he says, "The first startlingly authentic note was sounded by Claude McKay, a Jamaican Negro living in America." (p. 82) Then he mentions Countee Cullen, Langston Hughes, and refers to sociological factors, including "the powerful stimulation of the master dream-maker from the West Indies, Marcus Garvey." (p. 84) Johnson dwells, understandably, on the role of *Opportunity* magazine in the Negro Renaissance and on Alain Locke's involvement with both the magazine and the movement. Johnson saw the contribution of the movement as an enduring one and concluded:

> We have in this present period, and out of the matrix of the Renaissance period, scholars who know the cultural process, . . . and are aiding human knowledge, within the context, not of a

special culture group, but of the national society and world civilization. (p.88)

Sterling Brown, writing on "The New Negro in Literature," takes as his time span 1925-1955, and subdivides as follows:

1) The Harlem Vogue (1920-1930)
2) The Depression Thirties
3) World War II and Its Aftermath.

Brown did not mince words:

> I have hesitated to use the term Negro Renaissance for several reasons; one is that the five or eight years generally allotted are short for the life span of any "renaissance". The New Negro is not to me a group of writers centered in Harlem during the second half of the twenties. Most of the writers were not Harlemites; much of the best writing was not about Harlem. . . . The New Negro movement had temporal roots in the past and spatial roots elsewhere in America, and the term has validity, it seems to me, only when considered to be a continuing tradition. (pp. 57-58)

Brown held this opinion stoutly for the rest of his life; but the name Harlem was too seductive and won out. However, his perception of the New Negro movement as a continuing one which did not in fact terminate with the Harlem Boom of the 1920's is widely accepted. We may illustrate this from three notable anthologies. In 1972 the anthology *Black Writers in America*, edited by Richard Barksdale and Keneth Kinnamon, appeared. It offers as a major period "Renaissance and Radicalism" with the dates 1915 to 1945. In the same year, *Afro-American Writing: Prose and Poetry*, edited by Eugenia Collier and myself, covers the decade of the New Negro in a section headed "World War I to World War II." The long-awaited Norton Anthology, *African American Literature*, edited by Henry Louis Gates, Jr. and Nellie Y. McKay, appeared in 1997 and grandly uses the title "Harlem Renaissance" to embrace the years 1919 to 1940. The introduction to this section offers a nuanced rationale for the umbrella use of the term and states, curiously:

> Although it is convenient and even accurate to include Hurston's lyrical 1937 novel, . . . *Their Eyes Were Watching God*, within the boundaries of the movement, it is also clear that by that year the movement was absolutely finished. . . .  (p. 936)

To return however to the 1955 symposium, James Porter, who differed sharply, but politely, from Locke's analysis and dirigism in the realm of the visual arts, continued his dissenting reading in his essay, "The New Negro in Modern Art." He notes, however, that "there were but few Negro intellectuals who deliberately concerned themselves with Negro art in the 1920's and that only Alain Locke bothered to study and to write about its merits and promise." (p. 55) This follows by several pages his tart observation that "it had been Dr. Locke's hope as expressed in 'Legacy of the Ancestral Arts' [*The New Negro*] that the African tradition should serve as counteractive in Negro Art to the banalities . . . of our expression." (p. 52)

Here, just as we have noted the defeat of Brown's anti-Harlem campaign, we should note the triumph of Locke's ancestralism, attested in numerous art exhibitions of the last two decades. Already in 1970, I curated an exhibition of then-living artists in an exhibition *Homage to Alain Locke*, sponsored by the United Negro College Fund and the Center for African and African American Studies of Atlanta University. Among the artists included in the show, all of whom had known Alain Locke, were Romare Bearden, Beauford Delaney, Aaron Douglas, Palmer Hayden, Jacob Lawrence, Lois Jones Pierre-Noel, Alma Thomas, Charles White and Hale Woodruff.

In 1984, an exhibition, *A Blossoming of New Promises: Art in the Spirit of the Harlem Renaissance*, was held at Hofstra University. I was asked to contribute a preface to the catalog. What I wrote presents my thinking and a relevant part of the discourse concerning the Harlem Renaissance at that time.

The meaning of the Harlem Renaissance in the unfolding of American social history is still open to many interpretations. The phenomenon was itself varied and complex, multi-dimensional; its impact and its very existence have been disputed and even denied. But the continuing commotion and dissension are evidence that it was something fiber-deep in the warp and woof of Afro-American life.

The period following World War I in the United States is delineated differently, depending on whose social history you read. For the sensitive, young, white American artist, it was a period of disillusionment following a gross and inexplicable carnage. It was this select group which Gertrude Stein is alleged to have described as a Lost Generation, an epithet which acquired metaphoric force with F. Scott Fitzgerald as prime exemplar. For the great white American public it was a period of industrial expansion and consequent optimism. The automobile rolled off the factory lines, the motion picture industry, freshly ensconced in southern California, manufactured dreams, and positive noises emanated from a placid White House. One White House occupant spoke of "normalcy," another, who spent some of his time sliding down banisters, proclaimed, "the business of America is business."

From *Main Street* to *Dodsworth*, Sinclair Lewis was the derisive poet of this experience. Still another segment of white America abandoned itself to the Jazz Age, the roaring twenties, a mixture of fantasy, flappers, and prohibition booze. Carl Van Vechten is unjustly neglected as a delineator of this movement in his novels from *The Tattooed Countess* to *Parties*.

But what of Black America? Segregation alone would assure us that its involvement with these three currents would be distant. There is in fact a grim reality seldom mentioned, or perhaps not even realized by most dabblers in social history. Nearly half of the black population in the twenties was still locked in the poverty of the rural South and as cut off from what the social historians write about as if they were at the North Pole or in the Andes.

A breach in this fortress of deprivation had been made by the Great Migration from country to city and from South to North during World War I, and the migration continued throughout the twenties, creating the new classic ghettos of New York, Chicago, Philadelphia, and beginning those of other cities.

During this period, then, only half of Black America was involved in the urban mainstream of American life in some manner or the other, and half of this group (25% of the total) was in the urban South, fancifully called by H. L. Mencken, the Sahara of the Bozart, though less fanciful epithets may have been devised by those actually in residence there.

For the relatively Favored Fourth of Black America in the cities of the Northeastern and Central States, there was during the twenties a relatively optimistic and upbeat attitude about their prospects in American life.

More deeply than most, these Black Americans had been moved by the slogan of making the world "safe for democracy". While not accepting literally the glib phraseology of the moment, they hoped that some semblance of reality could be induced from the high sentiments. For those who had in fact escaped the grim fortresses of Dixie law and order and for others who had slipped the strait jacket of colonial caste in the West Indies, New York, Philadelphia, and Chicago seemed, if not a promised land, at least an oasis of promise. Hence, the mood of the Black America usually chronicled, that of this Favored Fourth, stands in marked contrast to that of the tiny Lost Generation or of the massive Main Street constituency.

The basic optimism reflected in James Weldon Johnson's *Black Manhattan,* a book which sums up the history of Black New York from the perspective of the twenties and which places great emphasis on the theatric dimension, is not far from the center of the mood of Black artists and intellectuals in New York and in other metropolitan centers. Further, I think that it is not too much to assert that alienation between this necessarily small group and the larger Black population of the cities did not exist, in the sense that such alienation is posited between the Lost Generation and Main Street.

The mood of optimism that permeates Johnson's work is based upon his perception of the growth of Harlem in the twenties as a viable cultural community with an intense life of its own which had become a center attracting international attention. A number of cosmopolite artists and thinkers boldly proclaimed that Harlem was where it was at, that Black creativity held the greatest promise for the renewal of the arts and that Harlem was the crossroads of this creativity, and the real capital, if you will, of the Black world.

Two major exhibitions, illustrative of Locke's influence, are documented in the 1986 catalog *Harlem Renaissance: Art of Black America* and the 1989 *Against the Odds: African American Artists and the Harmon Foundation.* Together they present an interacting body of commentary by David Driskell, Richard Powell, David Levering Lewis and others whose names are now mantras for the study of the Harlem Renaissance.

A series of events of particular importance to the development of the historiography of the Harlem Renaissance was initiated in 1957 with the founding of the *College Language Association Journal* by Therman B. O'Daniel at Morgan State College. This journal was understandably hospitable to articles treating all phases of Negro literature, as it was still then called. In 1961 *Negro Digest* (later to become *Black World*) was revived in Chicago under the editorship of Hoyt Fuller. In 1967 was launched the *Negro American Literature Forum* (subsequently the *Black American Literature Forum*) which metamorphosed into the *African American Review* in 1992. The publishing activity of these journals was supplemented by other periodicals, both new and old.

A notable event of 1967 was the publication of Harold Cruse's *The Crisis of the Negro Intellectual*, a thoroughly iconoclastic view of Black intellectual and political leadership. Cruse found little virtue in any of the icons of the Harlem Renaissance, and he could be quoted in condemnation of just about any figure who had crossed his mind, old Negro or New Negro, though he expressed a concern for plain, unmodified Negroes.

The year 1968 saw several re-publications of *The New Negro*; the Athenaeum reprint carried a preface by Robert Hayden, in which he said notably,

> The Negro Renaissance was clearly an expression of the Zeitgeist, and its writers and artists were open to the same influences that their white counterparts were. What differentiated the New Negro from other intellectuals was

their race consciousness, their group awareness
. . . (p. xi)

This observation of Hayden's had to wait more than three decades before it had major reverberations in the historiography of the Harlem Renaissance. However, as early as 1974 in an essay "The Outer Reaches" I explored the contribution which white writers made to the "blackening" of the twenties by their use of Black characters and subjects.

In the 1970's the pace of Harlem Renaissance studies accelerates, and two signature publications appear. In 1971 *Harlem Renaissance* by Nathan Huggins saw the light of day. This book played a major role in bringing the Harlem Renaissance to students and scholars. Among its outstanding achievements was the "outing" of the "Godmother" of Langston Hughes and Zora Neale Hurston, the rich primitivist, Charlotte Osgood Mason. Huggins's ultimate judgment on the Harlem Renaissance is measured and reserved:

> Taken all in all, it becomes easy to dismiss as mere vainglory the celebration of Harlem culture following World War I. On balance it appears that Wallace Thurman was more correct in his cynicism than Alain Locke was in his eager optimism. (p. 302)

Twenty-five years later such a judgment seems unnecessarily careful.

The very next year the amiable Arna Bontemps edited a collection, *The Harlem Renaissance Remembered* (1972). His own essay is entitled "The Awakening: A Memoir." Though based in large part on research, it is warm with reminiscences. He describes being drawn to

New York by the excitement of what appeared to be happening there:

> I came up out of the subway at 125th Street and Lenox Avenue and stood blinking in the sun. I didn't know anyone in New York, and the person to whom I had a letter of introduction had moved, or at least was not home. (p. 16)

Not long after he met Countee Cullen. Later Cullen invited him to a party to meet Langston Hughes. He was presented to Jessie Fauset, Charles S. Johnson, Alain Locke, and Eric Walrond, and eventually Hughes. Bontemps reflects:

> Thinking about that evening from this distance, I can't help contrasting it with the fictional highjinks contrived by Wallace Thurman . . . Thurman had arrived a year afterward but never became closely associated with those who gathered at this time to welcome the wandering poet . . . . (p. 19)

The Arna Bontemps collection includes the important essay by George Kent, "Patterns of the Harlem Renaissance" (p. 27), which had already appeared in the latter's *Blackness and the Adventure of Western Culture*. Kent felt it necessary to consider various reservations concerning the Harlem Renaissance, particularly those of Harold Cruse, but concluded "The Harlem Renaissance made paths through what had been stubborn thickets."

In 1973 appeared in English translation Jean Wagner's *Black Poets of the United States,* originally published in 1963 as a doctoral dissertation. Over two-thirds of this magisterial volume of more than 500 pages are devoted to "The Negro Renaissance," with chapters respectively on Claude McKay, Jean Toomer, Countee Cullen, James Weldon Johnson, Langston Hughes and Sterling Brown.  It is not without interest that this somewhat neglected study by a French scholar should have been the most solid study of its topic until that date, and in some respects is still not superseded.  Wagner states,

> The Negro Renaissance emerges in its entirety out of a new vision of the race's common past. . . . now the Negro labors to restore the true image of that history . . . . while engaged in rehabilitating his past, he also redeems his black color and all that it stands for.  For this is the visible sign that testifies to the common destiny uniting him with all other Negroes in the world, . . . (p. 161)

In this comment Wagner has leapt to a synthesis that would have been contested by virtually all critics on the Harlem Renaissance up until then, and which may be too much for most of them now.  Some would say that he has in fact defined the Black Arts Movement.  In February 1976 *Black World*, the organ of the Black Arts Movement, published an issue devoted to the Harlem Renaissance under Hoyt Fuller's editorship.

The eighties saw a veritable flood of works dealing with aspects of the Harlem Renaissance, led by David Levering Lewis's *When Harlem Was in Vogue* (1981).  Bustling, full of energy, and frequently irreverent, Lewis's book dared go where no one had gone before; it looked not only at events and publications and colloquies, but also at private life. Lewis is ever ready to posit sexual possibilities. Is the man in Jessie Fauset's poem

"La Vie C'est La Vie" real; is he—mirabile dictu—W. E. B. Du Bois? Well, Lewis doesn't say it is so, but the speculation is there to haunt and taunt the reader. Was Countee Cullen's adopted father, the Reverend Mr. Cullen, "a menace to the choir boys"? Well, it was so rumored. But one wonders if there were ever choir boys in a Harlem Methodist Church. Despite a penchant for "outing," Lewis provides a scintillating picture of the Harlem Renaissance, belying his dour conclusion that ultimately it was less than a success. The last chapter of his book is mournfully entitled "It's Dead Now."

In this chapter, he tells us:

> The Depression accelerated a failure that was inevitable, for the Harlem Renaissance could no more have succeeded as a positive social force . . . than its participants could have been persuaded to try a different stratagem of racial advancement. (p. 305)

In 1994, Lewis returned to the Harlem Renaissance as the editor of *The Portable Harlem Renaissance Reader.* He remained skeptical of its achievement, despite presenting an anthology of over 700 pages, 200 more than *The New Negro.* He opens the introduction with a conspiracy theory:

> The Harlem Renaissance was a somewhat forced phenomenon, a cultural nationalism of the parlor, institutionally encouraged and directed by the leaders of the national civil rights establishment for the paramount purpose of improving race relations in a time of extreme national backlash. . . .

Lewis had also developed a categorization of the Renaissance as follows:

> 1917-1923 Phase One. The Bohemian
> Renaissance
> 1924-1926 Phase Two. The Talented Tenth
> Renaissance
> 1926-1935 Phase Three. The Negro
> Renaissance.

At 1935 in his chronology we read "The Harlem Riot on March 19 marks the end of the Renaissance." (p. xlvii)

In 1982, a tool appeared which facilitated research and study of the Harlem Renaissance. This was Margaret Perry's *The Harlem Renaissance: An Annotated Bibliography and Commentary.* In 1976 Perry had written a survey of the Harlem Renaissance in *Silence to the Drums*, and in 1971 she had published a bio-bibliography of Countee Cullen. Another reference work saw the light of day in 1984: *The Harlem Renaissance: A Historical Dictionary for the Era*, edited by Bruce Kellner. The entries are by the editor and seven collaborators. This work of almost 500 pages astonishes by the fact that it exists. It is understandably quite uneven, dependent as it was almost entirely on secondary sources. It devotes articles to persons, places and things. Alberta Hunter is here as well as the Savoy Ballroom.

By the eighties, the rise of feminist and womanist studies fostered its own sequence of Harlem Renaissance studies. These include:

> Gloria Hull, *Color, Sex and Poetry: Three Women Writers of the Harlem Renaissanc*e (1987)

Maureen Honey, *Shadowed Dreams: Women's Poetry of the Harlem Renaissance* (1989)
Elizabeth Brown-Guillory, *Wines in the Wilderness: Plays by African American Women from the Harlem Renaissance* (1990)
Mary Knopf, *The Sleeper Wakes: Harlem Renaissance Stories by Women* (1993)
*Sisters of the Harlem Renaissance: The Found Generation, 1920-1932*, a postcard folder (1991)
Cheryl Wall, *Women of the Harlem Renaissance* (1995).

Two densely plotted and annotated studies illustrative of Robert Hayden's point about white-Black interaction appeared in 1995. Ann Douglas's *Terrible Honesty: Mongrel New York in the 1920's* attempts to locate Blacks in the cultural currents of the jazz age. George Hutchinson undertakes a more focused task in *The Harlem Renaissance in Black and White* and provides the most detailed reading of many aspects of white-Black literary and cultural interaction in the 1920's.

Also in 1995 in a series entitled "Circles of the Twentieth Century," Steven Watson offered an idiosyncratic and capricious handbook, *The Harlem Renaissance: Hub of African American Culture, 1920-1930.* The premise of the work is the following:

. . . Key moments of cultural transition are driven not only by the individual artists and writers . . . but also by a complex nexus of editors, patrons, critics. . . . (p. ix)

Hewing to its premise it includes such exotica as the "Colored Cabaret Owners Association Rules" and a chart entitled "Patrons, Mentors and Negrotarians."

Harlem Renaissance history, criticism, and documentation, all aspects of its historiography, show little sign of abating. Studies of individual figures, too numerous to mention, have followed in the wake of Robert Hemenway's biography of Zora Neale Hurston and the double-barrelled Langston Hughes biography of Arnold Rampersad. New books are announced or threatened constantly. The decade of the nineties has offered as many works on the Renaissance as have all preceding decades combined.

Of particular interest to Harlem Renaissance historiography is the recent intense activity among scholars in Europe, particularly France and Germany, in Harlem Renaissance studies. Under Michel Fabre and Genevieve Fabre at the University of Paris a number of theses and dissertations on the Harlem Renaissance have been produced. In 1998, two conferences on the Harlem Renaissance were held in France. In Germany a conference has been proposed on a European by-product of the Renaissance, the mega-anthology by Nancy Cunard called simply and perhaps threateningly, *Negro*.

It is appropriate to conclude this rehearsal for a historiography of the Harlem Renaissance with a brief account of a 1997 project originating at London's Hayward Gallery which enlisted the collaboration of the Corcoran Gallery of Art in Washington. The project was conceptualized and curated by David Bailey, a young English photographer/archivist and the African American art historian Richard J. Powell. Under the title *Rhapsodies in Black*, the project consisted of a traveling exhibition, a conference on the art, literature, and music of the Harlem Renaissance, and a range of ancillary materials including an information pack and a website.

A brief quotation from each of the curators will be indicative of the project. David Bailey states in the Introduction:

> *Rhapsodies in Black* is intended to challenge conventional representations of the Harlem Renaissance and to provoke new readings of the period from a contemporary perspective. For the first time, British and American writers and curators have joined together to explore this subject in a collaborative partnership to look at black and white relationships, and at ideas of nationhood and internationalism. (p. 11)

Richard Powell in his essay "Re/Birth of a Nation" looks back upon the fate and fortunes of Alain Locke's "little Renaissance" and says that

> . . . barely cold in its grave, [it] was resurrected by historians and critics and, like a jazz-age 'School of Athens', found its way into the history books and annals of a modern imagination. Indeed these Harlem Renaissance 'seeds' . . . became 'everlasting songs' and 'singing trees', growing strong, providing cultural sustenance and multiplying with each generation. As a late twentieth-century, post-modern emblem of black artistic genius and community, the visual, literary, performance, and ultimately conceptual dimensions of the Harlem Renaissance both illuminate a shadowy past and prescribe a brilliant future. (p. 32)

I accept these words of Professor Powell as a suitable coda to my ruminations.

# III

# Harlem Renaissance Conundrums and Jetsam

In the Burch lecture at Howard University, I attempted a sketch of a historiography of the Harlem Renaissance. The present undertaking is not so ambitious. Indeed, I have been encouraged to be relaxed and informal, even personal, and the result will be what may more properly be called a ramble, with a bow in the direction of what still remains a desirable enterprise—a formal inquest into the historiography of the Harlem Renaissance.

We may begin with the phrase itself—*the Harlem Renaissance*. Harlem? Renaissance? The term has become a short-hand designator for a variety of actors, actions, and events in African American literature and arts, perceived as being set into motion by the change in African American life precipitated by World War I and continuing until the onset of the Great Depression in the thirties.

In my book, *African Americans: A Portrait* (1993), I have designated this period as the onset of the trans-urban epoch of African American culture, characterized by the shift of African American life and sensibility from the rural South to the urban South and North, a period of intense activity manifesting itself in organizations and institutions of all kinds, as well as in an explosion of expressivity, particularly in popular culture. This vigor, amid the more sombre coloring of social oppression, is fully reflected in the energetic Black press of the time, an under-utilized mirror of the temper of the Black twenties.

That the term *Harlem* should be applied to a burgeoning national cultural upheaval has been contested by a few intransigent souls, notably Sterling Brown, poet and professor. Brown denounced the chauvinism of the Harlemites—most of them New Yorkers by adoption, and in the seminal anthology, *The Negro Caravan* (1941), of which he was senior editor, he allowed no such designation to seep through. We search *The Negro Caravan* in vain for any mention of a Harlem movement. Alain Locke's essay "The New Negro" is included and the introduction to it mentions the "Negro Renaissance" (p. 948).

In the introduction to "The Short Story" (p. 13) and to "Novels (Selections)" (p. 142), there are passing references to "the New Negro Movement". Most telling, however, in the introduction to "Poetry," we read:

> That Harlem was the Mecca of the New Negro movement is only natural, just as New York is the publishing capital of the nation. . . . And yet as Charles S. Johnson pointed out, *The New Negro* poets were by no means a Harlem school. Only McKay and Cullen were really Harlemites, and McKay was in Russia at the height of the movement.  (p. 281)

Referring to Sterling Brown himself, the passage continues:

> Brown's work belongs to the new regionalism in American literature; regionalism and social protest characterize his later poems. . . . (p. 282)

It is obvious that by 1941, when *The Negro Caravan* appeared, an insidious trend to replace the earlier term New Negro and Negro Renaissance was underway. It is hard to nail down precisely who was practicing this subversion, but it was clearly the wave of the future.

## Locke Looks Back

It was Alain Locke who, in writing the essay "The New Negro," had proclaimed a Renaissance on the pattern of the much heralded Irish Renaissance, centered in Dublin. Locke's enthusiastic exposition appeared in 1925.

In 1929 Alain Locke wrote the first of a series of retrospective annual reviews of what was to be called the "Literature of the Negro". Looking back on 1928, he remarks:

> The year 1928 represents probably the floodtide of the present Negrophile movement. More books have been published about Negro life by both white and Negro authors than was the normal output of more than a decade in the past. (*Critical Temper*, p. 201)

A note is sounded here to which we will return, that of the contribution of white writers to the pool of books with Black subjects.

Locke continued ominously,

> More aspects of Negro life have been treated than were ever dreamed of. The proportions show the typical curve of a major American fad, and to a certain extent, this indeed it is. (Ibid.)

Those novels of 1928 which he described as "really important events" were "Claude McKay's *Home to Har-*

*lem*, Rudolph Fisher's *Walls of Jericho*, and Julia Peterkin's *Scarlet Sister Mary.*" He also mentions Du Bois's *Dark Princess* and Nella Larsen's *Quicksand*, and observes "the veteran must . . . cede position in this field to the quite successful thrust of the novice. . . ." In theatre, 1928 was the year of the dramatization of *Porgy*, but also of a volume of plays, most with "Negro" subjects, by Paul Green. In 1928, there was the first of several Harmon Foundation traveling exhibitions of work by African American artists. Venues included the Art Institute of Chicago, the Harlem Branch of the New York Public Library, and Fisk and Howard Universities.

Locke did not write a retrospective review of 1929, but he did so for 1930, and for every year after until 1941, when they seem to have been interrupted by World War II. All of these reviews were published in *Opportunity*.

Reviewing 1930, Locke refers to the movement in the past tense:

> The much exploited Negro renaissance was after all a product of the expansive period we are now willing to call the period of inflation and overproduction. . . . (Ibid., p. 205)

The movement, in Locke's view, had failed to utilize its fundamental capital, and suffered from "the lack of any deep realization of what was truly Negro, and what was merely superficially characteristic." (Ibid., p. 206)

That Locke himself continued to mull over the possible failure of the movement is revealed in the retrospective review for 1938, entitled "The Negro: New or Newer." Observing that fifteen years had passed since "the literary advent of the 'New Negro,'" he asks the question, "do we confront today on the cultural front another Negro, either a newer Negro or a maturer 'New Negro'?" (Ibid., p. 271) Looking back on his own formulation of *The New Negro*, Locke declares that it was improperly realized by the figures of the twenties, but that a fuller comprehension of it was now in prospect. He does toss a bone to the older group, whom we may suspect is epitomized for Locke by Langston Hughes and Zora Neale Hurston. Locke remarks,

> Today we pivot on a sociological front with novelists, dramatists and social analysts in deployed formation. But for vision and morale we have to thank the spiritual surge and aesthetic inspiration of the first generation of artists of the renaissance decade. (Ibid., p. 273)

It is quite clear that for Locke, the Negro Renaissance was entombed in the twenties.

### Patrons and Primitives

One of the enduring clichés concerning the Harlem Renaissance is that it was characterized by a cohort of white patrons, much taken up with primitivism, who happily underwrote the frolics of various young Black artists who acted out the primitive expectations of their supporters.

On the roster of such patrons we find the names of Carl Van Vechten, Albert C. Barnes, the Harmon Foundation, Joel and Amy Spingarn, Nancy Cunard, and Charlotte Osgood Mason. There is also a roster of unmoneyed Blacks—shall we call them sub-patrons?—who were conduits of patronage. This list includes Alain Locke, Charles S. Johnson and Walter White. An anomaly was A'Lelia Walker, Black but with money.

Among the artists helped or corrupted by patronage we find the names of Langston Hughes, Zora Neale Hurston, Aaron Douglas, Richmond Barthe, Gwendolyn Bennett and Claude McKay. Other names float in and out of the shadows.

An attempt to concretise this myth occurs in a manual of the Harlem Renaissance compiled by Steven Watson in the "Circles of the Twentieth Century" series which offers a chart entitled "Patrons, Mentors and Negrotarians." (p. 96)

We may make short work of this web of patronage by noting first of all that athough most of these "patrons" had some money, they disbursed very little, and that Nancy Cunard, who lived in France, was rather poor and made only one foray into Harlem. The Harmon Foundation was principally a donor of prizes to winners of its art competition. Among the sub-patrons Walter White and Charles S. Johnson were zealous in their search for funds and opportunities for young artists, but their efforts had only modest success. The anomalous A'Lelia Walker was generous as a party giver and later went broke.

On the patron side, only Charlotte Osgood Mason deserves stellar treatment, with Alain Locke as her adjunct. Albert C. Barnes offers a side show.

In 1940, Langston Hughes published an autobiography, *The Big Sea*, narrating his life up until 1930. In a section late in the book, "Patron and Friend" (pp. 311-326), he tells us that while he was visiting New York on a vacation from Lincoln University, a friend took him to meet an elderly woman (she was about 75) who lived in great luxury on Park Avenue. He describes the luxury with some gusto. The gracious lady lavished money and gifts upon him. In time he developed a sense of unease as he contemplated the increasing poverty of Depression New York. He wrote a poem satirizing the opening of the Waldorf-Astoria from which his patron recoiled. Hughes decided, after having made a trip to Cuba at his patron's expense, that her expectations that he conform to her blueprint were untenable:

> So I asked kindly to be released from any further obligations to her, and she give me no more money, but simply let me retain her friendship. . . . But there must have been only the one thread binding us together. When that thread broke, it was the end. (p. 325)

Concerning the final scene with his patron and her response, Hughes said he could not write about it "because when I think about it, even now, something happens in the pit of my stomach that makes me ill." (Ibid.)

These lines were written nine years after the incident. Nathan Huggins reports in his *Harlem Renaissance* (1971) that Hughes at the end of his life (he died in 1967) "could not bring himself to talk about it without strong emotion." (p. 136) In his meticulous retracing of Langston Hughes's patron-primitive saga, Arnold Rampersad found it difficult to situate this episode and suspects Hughes of artistically telescoping a more complicated rupture. (p. 193ff.)

Significantly Hughes, in his account, never tells us the patron's name, holding fast to a promise. He does not tell us he was introduced to her by Alain Locke. Nor does he mention that there were fellow protegés.

Two years later Zora Neale Hurston in her autobiography *Dust Tracks on a Road* (1942) lets it all hang out. She introduces us to "Godmother, Mrs. R. Osgood Mason," and to other protegés: "She was Godmother to Miguel Covarrubias and Langston Hughes." This is the only mention of Langston Hughes in Hurston's autobiography and she does not mention Alain Locke in this connection.

In any case, it is my view that it is the pathological anecdote penned by Hughes concerning his relationship with Mrs. Mason which, elaborated and extended, has saddled Harlem Renaissance discourse with the patron syndrome. Not that Mrs. Mason is devoid of interest, since she also provided funding for Zora Neale Hurston, Alain Locke, Richmond Barthe, Aaron Douglas, Miguel Covarrubias and many others. However, she had been patronizing primitivism since early in the century, starting on the trail of Native American lore. It should be remembered that Covarrubias was a Mexican who eventually went off, probably with Mrs. Mason's support, to Bali. Apart from Hughes, no other of the protegés seems to have found the relationship traumatic.

The patronage which Dr. Albert C. Barnes offered to Aaron Douglas and Gwendolyn Bennett, two talented painters, was in the form of fellowships to attend the classes offered at the Barnes Foundation in Merion, Pennsylvania, where the curriculum was based on his theories of pictorial art, theories not generally shared by an art establishment against which he constantly battled. His hidden agenda in inviting these two African American artists is revealed in Douglas's account paraphrased in Amy Kirshke's *Aaron Douglas* (1995):

> One afternoon toward the end of the fellowship year Douglas and Bennett finally met with Barnes. . . . Barnes told the two Blacks that he wanted them to write a statement or essay attacking Alain Locke. When they asked him

what he wanted them to say, Barnes responded that he would provide them with all the material they needed. (p. 109)

In failing to fall in with this scheme, the two artists forfeited the second part of the Barnes fellowships of that epoch, a stay in Paris. However, Bennett had already spent a year in Paris and Douglas was to do so a few years later.

Alain Locke, very much in the middle of the patronage wars, is harshly condemned for his apparent Osgood machinations by Arnold Rampersad. After sympathetically deploring Langston Hughes's "pathetic enslavement," rationalizing Hurston's bizarre deceptions, and finding some excuse for Mrs. Mason in "cherished notions about Africa so novel for her class and race," Rampersad asserts:

> Only Locke's behavior was almost entirely reprehensible. For all his great learning he was a slippery character, too fond of intrigue and of the pleasures that Mrs. Mason's money assured. (p. 200)

David Levering Lewis is much more sanguine in assessing Locke, whom Lewis has dubbed "the Proust of Lenox Avenue," (p. 144):

> Locke's bondage to Charlotte Mason, despite patronizing lectures and occasional acts of rank tyranny, was more apparent than real. He walked a tightrope between obsequious accommodation to the old lady and nervous fidelity to his own beliefs, dissembling masterfully and taking the cash." (p. 154)

## The Van Vechten Factor

Related to the patron-primitive cliché in Harlem Renaissance discourse is what we may call the Van Vechten Factor. Carl Van Vechten, already a moderately successful light novelist, threw himself into the burgeoning Negro Renaissance and became an aficionado, indeed the archpriest of that tribe denominated Negrotarians by the neologist Zora Neale Hurston. Van Vechten was enthusiastic, energetic and interventionist. He was an inveterate party animal, giving and attending parties at what seems a furious rate. He wrote letters and notes, non-stop, and received missives by the bushel. An extraordinary amount of what we know about quotidian Harlem Renaissance activity comes from the correspondence of Van Vechten with his friends. And who were his friends? Prominent among them were Langston Hughes and Zora Neale Hurston, but also James Weldon Johnson, Walter White, Paul Robeson, and Ethel Waters. These were to be life-long friendships. Who were not his friends? Du Bois, Jessie Fauset, Benjamin Brawley, Countee Cullen, all kept their distance. The relationship with Alain Locke was a strained one.

From the distance-keepers there has developed the line that white folks, particularly Van Vechten, corrupted many of the young artists of the Harlem Renaissance by influencing them to celebrate loose morality and low-down life. Langston Hughes was the prime exhibit. Why had the young genius who penned "The Negro Speaks of Rivers" descended to the rancid wastes of the "Weary Blues"? The reply was the Van Vechten influence. Van Vechten denied, Hughes denied, but it was to no avail.

Van Vechten stood condemned because in 1926 he had communicated to the world his picture of a gin-soaked, sexually active Harlem in the novel *Nigger Heaven*. The novel had the temerity to become a best seller, spreading derogatory images of Harlem far and wide. Many who condemned the novel did not bother to read it. The title and the author were enough. There were those, Du Bois among them, who read it with deep disapproval. But there were defenders, including Hughes, James Weldon Johnson and Walter White. And indeed the novel is amusing, and, in this Age of Rap, inoffensive.

The Van Vechten factor, for one reason or the other, has virtually effaced Carl Van Vechten, the American cultural mover and shaker. His name surfaces only in Harlem Renaissance discourse, which is a disservice to American cultural history in general. There are two aspects of Van Vechten which are diminished in this overemphasis upon his presence in the Harlem Renaissance. First that he maintained and retained a deep interest in African American culture and African American personalities until his death in 1964. The second is that he was a crucial figure on the American cultural scene for over fifty years, beginning as a music critic for The New York Times in 1906.

We are informed by the entry in *The Harlem Renaissance: A Historical Dictionary for the Era* (1984) that he had been exposed to such talents as Sissieratta Jones, Ernest Hogan, Bob Cole, George Walker, and Bert Williams, while still a youth in Cedar Rapids, Iowa (p. 367). Hence he came early to his knowledge and appreciation of African American creativity on stage.

I have already indicated that Van Vechten remained a life-long friend to James Weldon Johnson, Hughes and Hurston. He also welcomed into his circle the snappish

George Schuyler and became the godfather of Schuyler's daughter, the pianist Philippa Duke Schuyler. He assiduously cultivated and offered advice and support to a host of Black artists who emerged in the thirties and forties. Beginning in the 1930's he pursued a program of photographic portrait documentation of African Americans of interest and distinction. The fruit of this activity may be viewed in Rudolph Byrd's *Generations in Black and White* (1993) and in a number of archives.

Van Vechten established the James Weldon Johnson Collection at Yale (1941), the George Gershwin Collection at Fisk (1944) and the Rose McClendon Collection at Howard (1946). He was responsible for the establishment of the Stieglitz Collection of American Art at Fisk (1949), a donation from Georgia O'Keefe, which received considerable attention in the traveling exhibition *To Conserve A Legacy* (1999).

As to his general status in American culture we have time to mention only a few things. As a literary critic he was involved in the resurrection of Herman Melville from obscurity; as a music critic, he was one of the first American admirers of Stravinsky; and as a literary friend, he was the literary executor of Gertrude Stein.

Van Vechten is considered to be America's first dance critic, a fact illustrated by a collection *The Dance Writings of Carl Van Vechten* (1974) and also America's first dance photographer, duly commemorated in *The Dance Photography of Carl Van Vechten* (1981). His gifts, including photographs, to the Performing Arts Division of the New York Public Library, mark him as one of he major benefactors of that institution.

Van Vechten's captivity in the Harlem Renaissance is one from which one would hope he will one day be released.

## Grown Deep

In 1998 I gathered together a number of essays which I had written on the Harlem Renaissance over the years. The volume was entitled *Grown Deep,* echoing the line from Hughes's "The Negro Speaks of Rivers": "My soul has grown deep like the rivers." I will rehearse rapidly several motifs which provide the substance and the rationale of that collection.

I observe in the first essay of *Grown Deep* that the Harlem Renaissance has moved from periphery to center in the mapping of American culture. This observation may be demonstrated from any of several indices. One could check the annual programs of the Modern Language Association (MLA) for examples. It is safe to assume that the Harlem Renaissance first appears there in the safe confines of sessions devoted exclusively to African American literature. The movement may now he invoked in almost any discussion of twentieth century American literature. A part of this voyage to the center is due to a recognition that the term *Jazz Age* applied contemporaneously to the twenties and maintaining its hold ever since is a signifier of the ubiquity of African American music and culture during the twenties and since. Another part of the movement from periphery to center is the weakening of the Black-white divide which makes it possible to appreciate the cosmopolitanism of the personalities of the Harlem Renaissance.

We may examine these two topics—music and cosmopolitanism—in more detail.

In the essay on writers and music in the Harlem Renaissance I examine various relations to music and musicians manifested by literary figures. W. E. B. Du Bois, a lover of music, provided an on-going chronicle of music in the pages of *Crisis* in which he names such interpreters as tenor Roland Hayes, bass Paul Robeson, and violinist Clarence Cameron White. Though Du Bois did mention W. C. Handy, he does not apparently ever refer to Louis Armstrong, Duke Ellington, or Bessie Smith. Ellington and Armstrong today are regarded as among the greatest treasures of American music, "beyond category," to cite a phrase associated with Ellington. The fact is that they achieved maturity within the precincts of the Harlem Renaissance and the retrospective realization of this fact itself has contributed to the mainstreaming of the Harlem Renaissance.

It is insufficiently realized that Alain Locke, the sage of the Renaissance, was highly attentive to blues and jazz. *In The Negro and His Music* (1936), he notes:

> Jazz is more at home in Harlem than in Paris, unless Paris imports Harlem to play, sing and dance it as she used to do; but beyond that jazz is more at home in its humble folk haunts even than in Harlem. (p. 73)

And Locke noted, in 1936:

> And when it finally comes to the blue ribbon of the fraternity, Ellington's band has usually received the expert's choice, although for a racier taste, Louis Armstrong has always had his special praise and rating. The Continental critics . . . conclude that Armstrong is the most phe-

nomenal jazz player of today but that Duke Ellington is the greatest jazz composer. (p. 98)

Among the creative writers of the Harlem Renaissance it is Langston Hughes who takes pride of place as an aficionado of the blues-jazz tradition. His creation of the blues poem as a literary counterpart to the blues song is testimony to his absorption in the music.

Zora Neale Hurston, whose name is so often coupled with that of Hughes, had an equally strong involvement with the music of the folk as well as with blues and jazz. But Hurston may also be invoked to demonstrate the cosmopolitanism of the renaissance, despite the identification with the folk that she cultivated, demonstrated and exploited.

In his rather vicious roman à clef *Infants of the Spring* (1928), Wallace Thurman displays Zora Neale Hurston as countrified "Sweetie Mae Carr," one of the denizens of "Niggeratti Manor." Years before, Hurston tells us in *Dust Tracks on a Road*, she had, under the sway of Lorenzo Dow Turner's tutelage at Howard, aspired to teach English literature, "discourse on the 18th century poets, and explain the roots of the modern novel." (p. 137)

The garbled account in *Dust Tracks* of Hurston's experiences traveling with a light opera company is sufficient to reveal that she acquired a considerable knowledge of European vocal music and of such figures as Caruso, Mary Garden, Geraldine Farrar and Schumann-Heink, all before her Harlem years. (pp. 116-7)

In *Grown Deep*, I include also an essay treating the involvement of white writers with African American subject matter during the twenties, an activity which had the effect of intensifying the impression of a Black presence on the American scene generally. I entitled the essay, "The Outer Reaches." It is interesting, though, that apart from Van Vechten and Paul Green, these writers had little or no contact with Black intelligentsia or the Harlem Renaissance proper. However, these authors and their relevant works are a matter of interest to the cultural historian, for these works had a reverberation among that cohort of writers and thinkers who constitute our Harlem Renaissance roster.

In 1920 Eugene O'Neill's *The Emperor Jones* was produced by the Provincetown Players.

> The play was thought to mark a new step in the treatment of the black man on the American stage. First of all, the black is clearly the protagonist; the role is virtually a monologue. The performance requires a tour de force of the actor, serving to indicate the high caliber of black dramatic talent. (*Grown Deep*, p. 56)

*The Emperor Jones* hung like a brooding presence over the twenties. References to it are frequent, and it was a mixed blessing:

> It is not without its limitation, however, from a black perspective. Brutus Jones is reduced from a swaggering bravo to a simpering hulk in twenty-four hours by atavistic superstition induced by the beating of drums in the forest. The implication is clear. Nevertheless, the positive features, particularly the central role it gave a black actor, was emphasized by most black commentators. (p. 57)

The actors associated with the role were successively Charles Gilpin, Jules Bledsoe and Paul Robeson. In the thirties, Robeson was to appear in a hyped-up film version. Already in 1923, however, Robeson had appeared in another Eugene O'Neill play, this on the taboo subject of intermarriage. Entitled *All God's Chillun Got Wings*, it was to have a rocky fate, liked by neither Blacks nor whites. A second playwright to exploit Black subject matter was Paul Green, whose *In Abraham's Bosom* won a Pulitzer Prize in 1927.

The work by a white author which inspired the affection of Blacks and whites was the novel *Porgy*, which appeared in 1925, the year of *The New Negro*. *Porgy* was subsequently dramatized into the successful play *Porgy* (1927) and was the basis of the most successful American opera, George Gershwin's *Porgy and Bess* (1935). Gershwin had first considered basing an opera on *Nigger Heaven*. It is fascinating to contemplate what such a work would have been.

Speaking of white writers who undertook Black subject matter I observe:

> The social position of the black and the mythic ideology which supported it would tend to inhibit such writers from leaving the well-established terrain on which the black played his simple and simple-minded destiny, an endless cycle of dancing and laughing, of joy and sorrow, of shooting and knifing, and occasionally of spectacular, back-breaking toil. (p. 63)

I will conclude this meander by referring briefly to the essay on Pan-Africanism in *Grown Deep*. The African allusion in the Harlem Renaissance is endemic. In the essay I attempt to simplify the examination of this African emphasis by postulating

> four streams of Pan-African thought and sentiment in the Harlem Renaissance: (1) the political, represented by the Pan-African Movement and the Pan-African Congresses; (2) the populist, represented by the Garvey Movement; (3) the cultural, represented by scholars; (4) the romantic, represented by poets and fictionalists. There is, of course, both overlap and merging among these categories. (p. 42)

There was also both condescension and hostility toward the various Pan-Africanisms, what one could call anti-Pan-Africanism. I take as the most outspoken representative of this current in the twenties George S. Schuyler, who in various writings slaps down Langston Hughes, W. E. B. Du Bois, and Marcus Garvey. Schuyler's article "The Negro Art Hokum" which appeared in *The Nation* in 1926 (reprinted in *The Harlem Renaissance Reader*, ed. David Levering Lewis, pp. 190-94) is a pyrotechnical display of hard-headed integrationism. But it is the reply of Langston Hughes which has held the field with its triumphant, if sentimental, pledge:

> We build our temples for tomorrow, strong as we know how, and we stand on top of the mountain, free within ourselves. (*Reader*, p. 95)

# Books Cited in Chapters II and III

Byrd, Rudolph. *Generations in Black and White: Photographs by Carl Van Vechten.* Athens: University of Georgia Press, 1993.

*To Conserve a Legacy: American Art from Historically Black Colleges,* with essays by Richard J. Powell and Jock Reynolds. Cambridge: MIT Press, 1999.

*The Harlem Renaissance: A Historical Dictionary for the Era,* ed. Bruce Kellner. Westport, Connecticut: Greenwood Press, 1984.

*The Harlem Renaissance Reader*, ed. David Levering Lewis. New York: Viking, 1994.

Huggins, Nathan Irvin. *Harlem Renaissance.* New York: Oxford University Press, 1971.

Hughes, Langston. *The Big Sea: An Autobiography* (repr.), New York: Hill & Wang, 1963 (1940).

Hurston, Zora Neale. *Dust Tracks on a Road.* "The restored text established by the Library of America." New York: Harper Perennial, 1996 (1942).

Kirschke, Amy Helene. *Aaron Douglas: Art, Race and the Harlem Renaissance.* Jackson, Mississippi: University Press of Mississippi, 1995.

Lewis, David Levering. *When Harlem Was In Vogue.* New York: Vintage Books, Random House, 1981.

Locke, Alain. *The Critical Temper of Alain Locke*, ed. Jeffrey C. Stewart. New York: Garland Publishing, Inc., 1983.

Long, Richard A. *African Americans: A Portrait.* New York: Crescent Books (Random House), 1993.

Long, Richard A. *Grown Deep: Essays on the Harlem Renaissance.* Winter Park, Florida: Four-G Publishers, 1998.

*The Negro Caravan,* ed. Sterling A. Brown, Arthur P. Davis and Ulysses Lee. New York: The Dryden Press, 1941.

*The New Negro,* ed. Alain Locke (repr.). New York: Atheneum, 1992 (1925).

*The New Negro Thirty Years Afterward.* Washington, D.C.: Howard University Press, 1955.

Perry, Margaret. *The Harlem Renaissance: An Annotated Bibliography and Commentary.* New York: Garland, 1982.

Perry, Margaret. *Silence to the Drums: A Survey of the Literature of the Harlem Renaissance.* Westport, Connecticut: Greenwood Press, 1976.

Rampersad, Arnold. *The Life of Langston Hughes,* Vol. I, 1902-1941. New York: Oxford, 1986.

Van Vechten, Carl. *The Dance Photographs of Carl Van Vechten,* selected by Paul Padgette. New York: Dance Horizons, 1981.

Van Vechten, Carl. *The Dance Writings of Carl Van Vechten,* selected by Paul Padgette. New York: Schermer Books (Macmillan), 1974.

Watson, Steven. *The Harlem Renaissance: Hub of African American Culture, 1920-1930.* (Circles of the Twentieth Century) New York: Pantheon Books, 1995.